bxjc
9/06

SCHOLASTIC
News
Nonfiction Readers

Piranhas and Other Fish

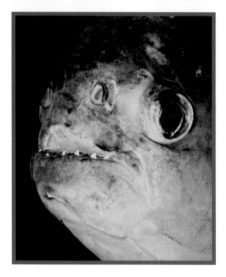

by
Mary Schulte

Children's Press®
A Division of Scholastic Inc.
New York Toronto London Auckland Sydney
Mexico City New Delhi Hong Kong
Danbury, Connecticut

These content vocabulary word builders
are for grades 1-2.

Consultant: William Fink
Professor of Ecology and Evolutionary Biology
University of Michigan
Ann Arbor, Michigan

Curriculum Specialist: Linda Bullock

Special thanks to Omaha's Henry Doorly Zoo

Photo Credits:

Photographs © 2005: Corbis Images: back cover, 13 (John Madere), 5 top left, 7 (Lawson Wood); Nature Picture Library Ltd./Georgette Douwma: right cover inset; NHPA/Ernie Janes: 23 top right; Photo Researchers, NY: cover background (Hans Reinhard/OKAPIA), 20, 21 (Dave Roberts/SPL); Seapics.com: center cover inset (Phillip Colla), 2, 4 bottom right, 5 bottom left, 5 top right, 8, 9, 17 (Mark Conlin), 23 bottom right (Bob Cranston), 1, 5 bottom right, 10 (Gregory Ochocki), left cover inset, 4 bottom left, 14, 15, 23 top left (Doug Perrine), 4 top, 19 (Andre Seale), 23 bottom left (Ron & Valerie Taylor); Visuals Unlimited/Ken Lucas: 11.

Book Design: Simonsays Design!

Library of Congress Cataloging-in-Publication Data

Schulte, Mary, 1958-
  Piranhas and other fish / by Mary Schulte.
    p. cm. – (Scholastic news nonfiction readers)
  Includes bibliographical references and index.
  ISBN 0-516-24932-0 (lib. bdg.) 0-516-24791-3 (pbk.)
  1. Fishes–Juvenile literature. 2. Piranhas–Juvenile literature. I. Title.
    II. Series.
  QL617.2.S38 2005
  597–dc22
                                                    2005002083

CHILDREN'S PRESS and associated logos are trademarks and or registered trademarks of Scholastic Library Publishing. SCHOLASTIC and associated logos are trademarks and or registered trademarks of Scholastic Inc.

1 2 3 4 5 6 7 8 9 10 R 14 13 12 11 10 09 08 07 06 05

CONTENTS

WORD HUNT

Look for these words as you read. They will be in **bold**.

angelfish
(**ayn**-juhl-fish)

gill slit
(gil slit)

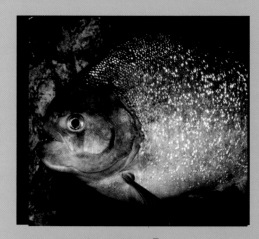

piranha
(pih-**rahn**-uh)

4

catfish

(**cat**-fish)

fin

(fin)

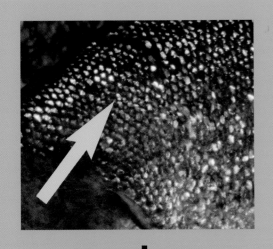

scales

(skales)

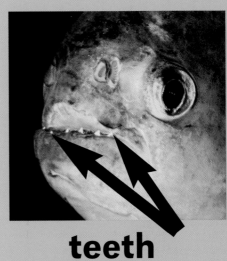

teeth

(teeth)

5

Fish! Fish!

Have you seen a perch, **catfish**, or trout?

All of these animals are fish.

Fish live in water.

Catfish are fish.

Some fish have **scales**.

This **piranha** has
many scales.

Scales protect the piranha.

As the piranha grows, its
scales grow, too.

scales

The piranha lives in the waters of South America.

Its **teeth** look like teeth on a saw.

They are as sharp as a saw's teeth, too.

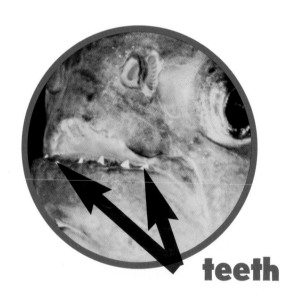

teeth

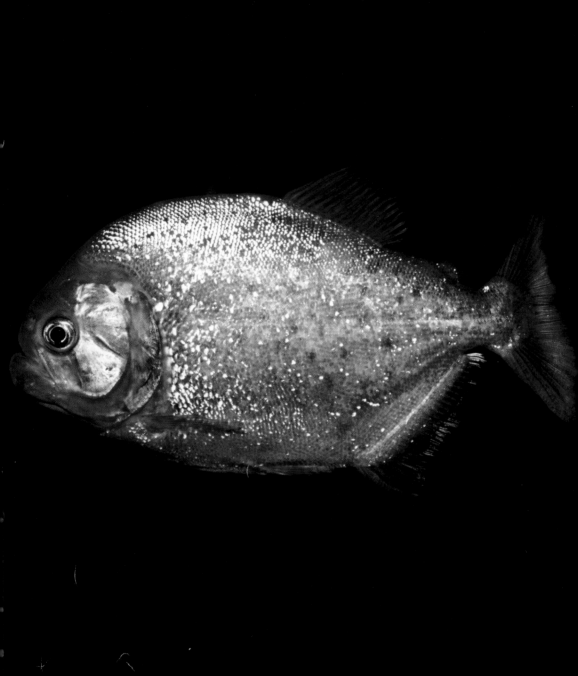

Piranhas hunt for food in the daytime.

They eat animals that are weak, hurt, or sick.

They rip flesh off fish, birds, and lizards.

Some piranhas eat seeds and fruit.

Look! One of these piranhas is eating a fish.

A shark is a fish, too.

Fish have gills.

Fish use gills to breathe underwater.

Gill slits are openings to the gills.

gill slit

Do you see the shark's gill slits?

Fish have **fins.**

The clownfish moves its tail fin back and forth.

This helps it move forward.

fin

fin

fin

Clownfish live in the ocean.

Angelfish are fish, too.

Fish are cold-blooded.

Their body temperature changes to match the water temperature.

When the water is cold, angelfish are cold.

When the water is warm, angelfish are warm.

PARTS OF A FISH
Here is an X-ray of a piranha.

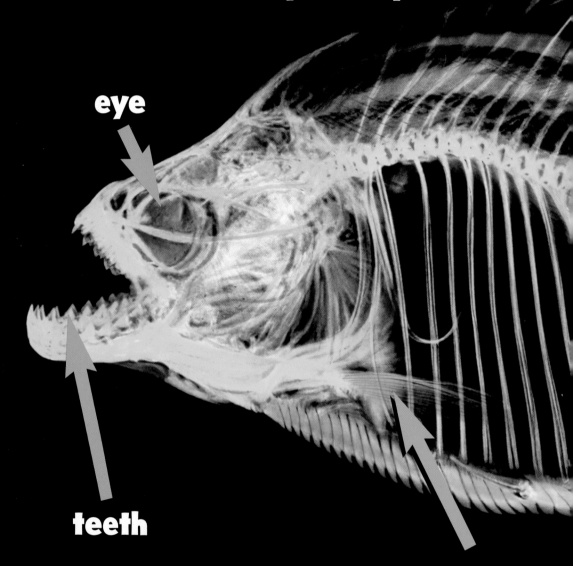

eye

teeth

fin

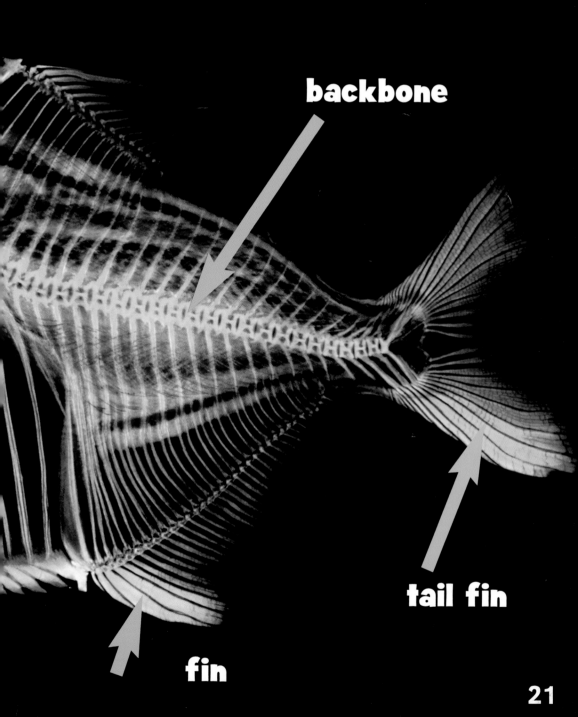

backbone

tail fin

fin

YOUR NEW WORDS

angelfish (**ayn**-juhl-fish) a brightly
colored fish that lives in warm water

catfish (**cat**-fish) a fish that lives in
freshwater and has whiskers around
its mouth

fin (fin) a body part of a fish shaped like a
flap that helps it move

gill slit (gil slit) gill slits cover a fish's gills

piranha (pih-**rahn**-uh) a small fish with
sharp teeth that lives in South America

scales (skales) small pieces of skin that
cover the bodies of some fish

teeth (teeth) hard, sharply pointed parts in
the mouth that are used to eat

IS IT A FISH?

Dolphin
(No. It's a mammal.)

Newt
(No. It's an amphibian.)

Sea snake
(No. It's a reptile.)

Whale
(No. It's a mammal.)

INDEX

FIND OUT MORE
Book:
Fishes: A True Book by Melissa Stewart (Children's Press, 2001)

Website:
http://www.enchantedlearning.com/classroom/quiz/fish.shtml

MEET THE AUTHOR:

Mary Schulte is a newspaper photo editor and author of books and articles for children. She is the author of the other animal classification books in this series. She lives in Kansas City, Missouri, where she is glad that piranhas do not inhabit the water.